Icy

By Juniata Rogers

The air is too warm for snow.
The ground is too cold for rain.
Look out! It is going to get icy!

Icy weather can be beautiful and dangerous.

Drivers must scrape their windows in icy weather.

Icy weather happens when the **temperature** is near 32 degrees Fahrenheit (FAYR-en-hyt). If it gets colder, snow is likely. Much warmer, and it will rain.

Icy weather takes many forms. **Sleet**, **hail**, and **freezing rain** are three kinds of icy weather.

Hail can be small like peas or bigger than golf balls!

Sleet is very slippery. It can be dangerous to walk on.

Sleet starts in a cloud as snow. On the way to the ground, it falls through warm air and melts a little. Then it hits cold air again. It refreezes as sleet.

In hailstorms, ice balls fall instead of rain. Hail is made in thunderstorms. Hail can fall in any season because the tops of thunderclouds are very cold.

Large hail can cause damage to cars and houses.

Freezing rain covers everything it touches with ice.

Freezing rain is water that is as cold as ice. It is rain when it falls. It freezes as soon as it lands.

When moist air freezes, it forms **frost**. Frost makes feathery patterns on doors and windows. When the sun hits frost, it melts away.

Frost covers a rose and its leaves.

Drivers must be very careful in freezing fog.

Freezing fog leaves frost and ice everywhere. Roads get slick, and the fog is hard to see through. It is a bad time for driving!

In an **ice storm**, ice builds up on roads and trees. The ice is heavy. It pulls down trees and power lines.

Heavy ice has caused these trees to bend over.

Freezing rain covered this forest in ice.

Ice can be dangerous. But it can be beautiful, too. Trees and grass sparkle like jewels. What do you do when it is icy outside?

Glossary

freezing fog (FREEZ-ing FAWG): Fog that forms on a freezing day and leaves ice on the ground.

freezing rain (FREEZ-ing RANE): Rain that is as cold as snow when it falls. It turns to ice in a flash when it hits the ground.

frost (FRAWST): Ice crystals that form when the water in moist air freezes.

hail (HAYL): Pellets of ice that form during thunderstorms.

ice storm (EYSS STORM): A storm in which a thick layer of ice builds up on roads and trees.

sleet (SLEET): Slushy ice that starts as snow, melts a bit on the way to the ground, and refreezes.

temperature (TEM-pur-chur): How hot or cold something is.

To Find Out More

Books

Black, Vanessa. *Ice Storms.* Minneapolis, MN: Jump!, 2017.

Jensen, Belinda. *Raindrops on a Roller Coaster: Hail.*
Minneapolis, MN: Millbrook Press, 2016.

Lawrence, Ellen. *How Are Rain, Snow, and Hail
Alike?* New York, NY: Bearport, 2012.

Websites

Visit our website for links about ice:
childsworld.com/links

Note to Parents, Teachers, and Librarians: We routinely verify our Web links to make sure
they are safe and active sites. So encourage your readers to check them out!

Index

About the Author

Juniata Rogers grew up in Newport, Rhode Island. She has worked as a naturalist, an art model, and a teacher. She's been writing professionally for 25 years, and currently lives near Washington, DC.

The Child's World®
childsworld.com

Published by The Child's World®
1980 Lookout Drive • Mankato, MN 56003-1705
800-599-READ • www.childsworld.com

Photo credits: ArtBitz/Shutterstock.com: cover, 1; Ben Romalis/Shutterstock.com: 11; chris kolacza/Shutterstock.com: 20; Gabor Tinz/Shutterstock.com: 7; Irina Mos/Shutterstock.com:19; Mikhailas/Shutterstock.com: 12; Paul Aniszewski/Shutterstock.com: 15; ratmaner/Shutterstock.com: 4; sevenke/Shutterstock.com: 3; Steve Allen/Shutterstock.com: 16; stockphotofan1/Shutterstock.com: 8

ISBN Hardcover: 9781503827882
ISBN Paperback: 9781622434565
LCCN: 2018939782

Printed in the United States of America • PA02398